73

MORE PRAISE FOR I NOW PRONONUCE YOU

Caroline Earleywine's first full-length collection *I Now Pronounce You* triumphantly claims her unapologetic and un-silenced space in the literary canon. Poem after poem is a symphony of her own hard-earned songs—as survivor, queer woman, daughter, wife, teacher bravely holding space for LGBTQIA+ youth in a hate-prone country. Moving through scenes that jump from past to present, from her parents' marriage to her own—while navigating an identity of silence and fear—Earleywine breaks through generational patterns and heals those she holds dear with her unflinching voice. She sheds so many skins within these pages, and becomes more and more seated in her truest self—"If my fear was a liar. If our love was a nesting doll we kept opening, if we kept becoming more of ourselves." She takes her wife's hands and with their fingers, strums the violin in her own heart with a braver song, "a braver life."

— Kai Coggin, author of *Mother of Other Kingdoms* and *Mining for Stardust*

I Now Pronounce You

by Caroline Earleywine

Write Bloody Publishing

writebloody.com

First edition.
ISBN: 978-1949342550

Cover Design by Derrick C. Brown
Interior Layout by Nikki Steele
Edited by Sam Rose Preminger
Proofread by Wess Mongo Jolley
Author Photo by Jenn Terrell photography

Type set in Bergamo.

Printed in the USA

Write Bloody Publishing
Los Angeles, CA

Support Independent Presses
writebloody.com

To my parents

and to Bonnie

I Now Pronounce You

I Now Pronounce You

Prelude

I.
Something Borrowed

II.
Something Blue

III.
Something New

Recessional

"Your silence will not protect you."

—Audre Lorde

"If we want the rewards of being loved we must submit to the mortifying ordeal of being known."

—Tim Kreider

PRELUDE

How She Loved Us

Cats had short life spans
in our house. Not soft deaths,
but loud accidents splayed
across our driveway.

When the garage door
strangled our tabby,
my mother left the house.
Returned with ice cream.

When she ran over
our calico cat we both saw,
but she kept driving.
Turned up the radio.

The surviving cats left
dead birds on our front porch.
Mom said they were gifts.
Meant they loved us.

She was the kind of woman
who saved cigarettes for after
we went to bed. Kept wine
in her closet.

When Dad moved
to the upstairs bedroom,
I asked why. "It's because
he snores," she said.

The weekend Mom took us
on a surprise trip to the river,
we came home and discovered
an empty house.

No blue truck in the driveway,
no razor by the sink, no ugly
ties in the closet. My mother
went out back

to water plants. She held
a bloody silence in her mouth.
Dropped it off, a lifeless bird,
on our front step.

I.

SOMETHING BORROWED

OUR FAVORITE GAME

We neighborhood girls loved to play
wedding, first with my little sister
and the neighbor boy. She wore a plastic
tiara and held yellow daffodils we'd picked
from the yard. The two of them looked wary
as we struck our toy instruments to march
them down the deck steps. Next, a young
neighbor girl and our little brother.
The sidewalk to our front door
was a perfect aisle, long and inviting.
But she cried and refused, no matter
how we tried to persuade her.
The show had to go on, so I stepped in
with my favorite dress-up gown.
There were no boys close
to my age in our neighborhood,
so my brother remained the little groom.
It was more about the ceremony of it
anyway, that we played our parts.
It went so well that Mom left
and returned with McDonald's
for the reception. That was the year
Mom planned to start work again as a nurse.
On her first day back, my brother broke
his arm. She took it as a sign to stay
home. To play her part. We ate our feast
of chicken nuggets at the picnic table, toasted
to what good women we were learning how to be.

THE ONLY GIRL OUT
AT MY HIGH SCHOOL

wore a lot of black. Her pants
were wide and bedazzled

with chains. She had a lip ring.
Wore a rainbow of bracelets

stacked to her elbow. I remember her
walking down the hall with two girls,

and I wondered if one was her love.
I wondered if it was lonely, being a stereo

of pride, bass booming, intimidating
and loud and all of the things girls weren't

supposed to be in that small Arkansas town
where kids debated over religion between classes,

said women are supposed to be silent
and gay people were going to hell.

My parents told me to take a walk,
not a stand, and I mostly listened.

Slow danced at prom
with my own shadow. My face,

a bouquet of scarlet anytime
my name was called in class.

I was a violin with the strings
plucked out, a symphony

of silence, exactly who
I was taught to be.

She was her own marching
band, parading down the halls

and even the religious ones
respected her. Liked her taste

in music. I once sat with her
on an empty stage after play practice

and watched her go through a playlist
on her laptop. I don't remember

the songs, but I remember we laughed.
I remember the way I felt

awkward, but also excited. How I paid
attention. Like I was hearing an overture,

collecting the melodies
so someday

I could sing them.

ON BEING A CLOSETED TEACHER

It's driving to school practicing what you'll say
if they ask you outright. It's reading the news
of a teacher fired after showing her class

a picture of her wife. It's smiling at the queer
student wearing a rainbow shirt and feeling

shame at your silence. It's overhearing
the teacher next door talk about her husband,
her family, her opinion on gay marriage:

"I just refer to the Bible on that one," she tells
her class. It's the teacher saying, "I just wouldn't

want my students thinking about my sex life," though
the picture of her husband on her desk is not
deemed inappropriate. It's feeling that you

are inappropriate. It's students yelling "Trump train!"
as they walk into your classroom the day after

the election. It's trying to keep your face neutral
as you tell them to settle down. It's living in the pause
after a student says, "Hey, can I ask you

a question?" It's holding your breath. It's living on
a stage, worrying that one day, you'll forget your lines.

The First Time

after he'd begged all night / for me to take / back my / no / and the sun slipped / into the window / he rolled / me over / I parted my legs / to the inevitable / watched him wear nothing / but me / I remember looking down / at our bodies / thinking / we looked like animals / he / this stranger / a dog / grunting in my ear / me / more like the fish / shipwrecked / on land / when he finally noticed / I was shaking / he stopped / held me / told me / it didn't count / since neither one of us / finished / at the doctor's that week / they swabbed me / for diseases / applauded me / for taking / the pill the next day / for coming in / said I'd done all / the right things

Magic Tricks

My mother's body was full
of trapdoors. For years she bled
remnants of siblings I would never

meet, let surgeons pry her open
like a fist that never held the missing
prize—cursed her body for not

performing its most impressive
trick. When I appeared
two years after my older sister

was adopted, they assumed
I was the flu. I have never
seen my parents kiss. The closest

memory I can conjure, a morning
Dad was kissing us all goodbye
on the cheek. My sisters and I

requested he give my mother
a *real* kiss. "Yes," my mother agreed,
leaning toward him, "give me a real kiss."

There was a frozen moment
while he hesitated. In the audience,
we held our breath. Then my father

gave my mother a quick peck
on the cheek and disappeared
before he could see her eyes

fall. I wondered which was worse:
to be the one denied magic, or the one
who forgot how to give it.

WHAT SEPARATES US

Our parents bathed
the four of us together,
a tub full of kids who
giggled and played,
didn't care when
the water got too
cold. When puberty hit,

> my little sister and I started
> showering on our own. We'd turn
> on music, sing along, suds
> crowning our heads. We'd talk
> and talk as we shaved our legs,
> just two years separating
> her preteen stubble from mine,
> a world that must have seemed
> so foreign

> to our brother, the only
> boy. Youngest and most
> lonely, who would sometimes
> sit on the other side
> of the closed door like
> a spy, or visitor who would
> never have such a home.

A Lesson on Tenderness

The woman down the street
walks her dog five times a day.
They walk slowly, allowing
the dog, whose name is Rooster,
to stop and smell every blade
of grass, or to roll on his back
in a yard, or to stare
at a neighbor unloading
groceries, longing
to be petted. I have stepped
out of my car to find him
waiting for me at the edge
of the yard many times,
his hair sprinkled with flecks
of white to match his human's,
his one eye staring intently
at me, the other lid stitched
together like the patchwork
of the most lovingly
sewed quilt. He often sits
on my feet when I pet him,
as if in effort to keep me
longer. Sometimes the woman
stands idle with him
for long minutes
as he stares
at a house he knows
holds a friend,
not daring to deny
him affection, or hope
or the possibility
of joy.

THE WORLD'S SMALLEST PRIDE PARADE

The day they legalized marriage for everyone—even
for two women, even in Arkansas—we were in our

kitchen. There was no champagne, no confetti,
but we did throw the world's smallest Pride parade

there among our dirty dishes, our dogs' necks adorned
with rainbow bandanas, fairy wings and tutus freed

from the darkest corners of the closet. The only music
was our own claps and squeals as we kissed and fell

to the cool tiles on that hot summer day. So much
didn't change, but our plans of moving to a state

more blue were shelved. Buying a ring became
a plan, not a wish. Enough changed that when

we walked to a last-minute celebration at a bar,
we did what we were so often afraid to—

we laced our fingers together, in broad daylight,
and walked down the street.

WHY I CAN NEVER CALL IT _____

Because he didn't hold me down.
Because I returned the kiss.
Because I drank the beers.
Because he seemed sorry after.
Because I said no but didn't repeat it.
Because it happened to my friends.
Because I thought it was normal.
Because it happened again. And again.
Because he stopped once I was crying.
Because I went back to him.
Because it can't be changed.
Because a name is powerful.
Because once it's named it can't be unnamed.

The Perfect Weapon

My silence holds brass
knuckles close
fisted in its pocket.

My silence is one hundred stories
tall. My silence took
the stairs, isn't even winded.

My silence can hold
its breath longer
than you.

My silence lives
in the closet, is the noosed
tangle of shoelaces.

My silence stains white
sheets, ghosts its finger-
prints on fogged mirrors.

My silence is an icicle. Sharp
as truth. Melts in my
own chest.

I Now Pronounce You

Many nights I dream about weddings.
I am almost always wearing the wrong

thing—hair and makeup disheveled,

showing up right before the ceremony,
not sure where the ring is. There is never

enough time—I am always frantic as I rush

home to retrieve the dress in the right
color, or throw together a suit, or do my hair,

or pin together the fabric that doesn't fit

my body. There are pictures, and I don't want
to stamp into memory this panic, to disappoint

the audience, the expectant crowd who turn

their heads when I burst through the church
doors, and why is it always a church? My wife

is often there, but sometimes it is just me

standing at the end of the aisle, trying
to marry some version of myself

I never knew how to be.

Dearly Beloved

As our family walks
down the church aisle
everyone stands as if
we are brides.

The preacher says
pretty words, speaks
of my aunt in the past
tense. No one objects.

My father wilts
beside me. No one
takes a picture
as we leave.

At the reception
there's no dancing.
There are flowers,
but no one throws

a bouquet. We don't
want to know
who's next.

Broken Ghazal
After Suzanne Langlois

Maybe needles are slivers of light kissing your body.
Maybe X-rays are portraits of outer space, the body

a galaxy—maybe the tumor is a Mona Lisa moon.
Maybe it's beautiful. Maybe cancer is a body

trying to live forever, cells in frantic creation—
a big bang. Maybe my aunt is somebody

not cremated, but confettied, my uncle, the guest
who shows up six months late, after everybody

has gone home. Maybe my grandmother's urn is the bottom
half of an hourglass, years collected in a bronze body.

Maybe my grandfather's stomach wasn't filled with cancer,
but with stars, a whole night sky he swallowed when nobody

was looking. Maybe this sickness isn't in me, or my siblings
or parents, or if it is, it's not the slow-moving guillotine, body

as bomb, undetonated. Inevitable. Maybe it's just
lonely. Maybe it thinks of itself as a friend, somebody

who will walk up to me on the street one day and say
"Caroline, it's me! It's so good to see you." Maybe bodies

are stars in a constellation, dead long before the light reaches
us. Maybe we look up   and see

them   dots
          we   connect
pieces   of the same
                        broken

                                        body.

I Don't Believe in Time Travel

but last night at a bar   surrounded

      by queer women   dancing   he

walked in   pushed   between us   belly first

      spidered   his hands toward bodies

not wanting   to be   touched   and it was not

      my ass   in his hand   not my waist

he held   like the neck   of a beer bottle but all at once

I was back   in the years   when that was just

      Friday Night   or The Man Who Found Me

Drunk At The Party   and Took Me

      Home   We swarmed the man   touching

our friend   with our "Don'ts"   and our hands

      pushed him   out of the bar   We high-fived

each other   over our beers   I told myself

we had won   something   but for days

      I am still there   the years of hands   taking

the strange surrender   of my body   I can't go back

      to reclaim it   Now I have names

for all those things done   in the dark.

Divorce

We found out through the newspaper.
Or rather, the mother of my sister's friend

asked how my sister was doing, having read it
with her morning coffee. My sister returned
home to deliver the news no one else had—

that the two-year limbo of my parents'
separation was over, that it was written

right there, in black and white.
What's that riddle about newspapers?
What's black and white and read

all over? When you see it spelled out
in writing, the answer becomes clear.

I Could Lose You

I could lose you as we sit across
from each other in some sterile
office, sign papers that undo
the vows we made, an invisible

braid of years between us un-
raveling despite all our therapy
and good intentions, or how hard
we tried. I could lose you if we grow

apart. If our desires and our love
change so much, we no longer
fit. If, despite all our best efforts,
we hurt each other in some irrevocable

way. A secret lover. The cold shoulder.
Each night, backs facing each other
in the bed we come to only share
out of habit. I could lose you

in an unsolved mystery where
I wake up and you are gone,
no trace of your dimpled chin
or laughter—years of searching

and uncertainty. The plane that flies
through the Bermuda Triangle.
Your car abandoned on the side
of the road. I could lose you in a grocery

aisle, and often do, your momentary
fascination with the pickle selection
or yogurt nutritional facts, or at a crowded
party, or when I meet you at a restaurant

and, for a few wild moments, can't find
your face among the tables. But what
is certain is someday, I will lose you
through death. That one of us will bury

the other. I can't stop thinking that to love is to carry this truth like a bruise, to hope that one day we will say, "It was worth it. Of course. I would do it all over again."

GOLDEN SHOVEL IN WHICH I QUESTION
THE INTEGRITY OF WRITING ABOUT MY FAMILY
after Lucille Clifton

Beneath every word I write, they
        stare up at me. How can I ask

my parents to let me
        tell our truths when it's going to

hurt them? To remember
        my story, can I not help but

hunt for the shadows they
        hide, the moments they don't want

inspected, and pull them toward me
        into the light? The truth is I have to

look so closely to remember
        who I am. The truth is even their

most painful memories
        are buried love poems, and

I keep on digging. I
        am not a god, but I keep

creating worlds. Is there room on
        the shovel for all of us? For remembering

which truth is theirs, which truth is mine?

ODE TO MY FOREHEAD WRINKLES

The rake's trail across sand. The reason I got bangs—
no lotion or pulling can smooth you. My grandmother
told me not to rub my eyes where skin is paper

delicate, like a crumpled napkin that can't be
straightened back out, but she never warned me
of you. I wonder if it is genetics, time making

its mark too soon, or if it's the years of wearing
my thoughts on my face like a banner: The scrunched
thinking face, the brows raised in surprise or scrutiny.

All the times I couldn't or wouldn't say how I felt,
you were there to display my feelings like a marquee,
your deep lines, letters etched into skin. You are proof

that even through my silences I spoke, that my feelings
earned their signatures across the page of my face,
that some stories can't stay inside the body.

II.

SOMETHING BLUE

Spring Cold Snap

At the first blush
of redbud trees,

when we've put away
our coats, basked

in the green, winter
snaps back. Wisteria

weeps, shivers
on its vines.

We cover our
flowers, whisper

beneath the bags
that the frost will

pass. Promise
sun, and hope

they believe us.

"Are You Gay?"

A pause. The class-
room stills, a single
drop from a blue

sky. I choose words
to make the smallest
ripples, say it's not

okay to demand
an answer, some
people aren't safe

if outed, or aren't
ready. And then,
"Yes, I am." A flood

of students' hands
in the air, questions:
"Do you have

a partner?"
"Have you ever
been bullied?"

"When did you
know?" Fourteen-
year-olds' eyes

wide and curious
as I answer some,
and gently draw

a boundary with
others, my voice
as steady as I

can manage.
One boy puts
his head down

as his shoulders
shake with
laughter. I start

to doubt, to regret
my honesty. I wonder
if I made a mistake.

After the bell rings,
they linger
at their desks

before approaching
me, the ones
who say, "I am

too," and "That
was brave," and
"Thank you." Words

that sink into
the darkest
parts of me.

A well
I drink from
again and again.

Interview with a Teacher in a Pandemic

1. How many feet apart are your desks?

Take the height of the boy who held
the belt wrapped around the doorknob
in the lockdown drill. Subtract ten
years. Subtract the number
of pages in the last
book he read that he
did not see himself
in. Subtract the mask
crumpled in
the school
hallway.
Subtract.
Sub-
tract.

2. What made you think you had control?

The metronome of my steady heart. My two good
hands. My classroom filled with books that once were
trees that once were seeds in the ground, in the safe,

dark earth—roots that spread like fingertips of an outstretched
hand, an inversion of the structure above it—the upside-down
world that only looks wrong if you don't know any better.

3. What did the school give you for protection?

My two
good hands.

4. How are you practicing self-care?

In the parking lot, teachers

sit in their cars before

school. We take

deep breaths, close

our eyes, will

ourselves to go

inside. We put on

our masks.

5. *To quote our governor, are you "bent out of shape?"*

I am a wire hanger   straightened

     to needle.   I am a contortionist,

my every limb   displaceable.   See

    how I bend,   see how I don't

   even look   like a body

          at all?

Sylvia Speaks to Me

Patron saint of sad girls who've fallen
in love with their sadness. Dead

glitter of dew, obscene engine
of madness—is that how

you see me? It's so much
more than that. This capacity

to feel. To say it, freely, to not pretty
up a goddamn thing. Funny how

my words were once your bible.
Now, my name is your

computer password. An homage
to your past, a throwback

to teen angst. You think that sad girl
isn't still inside you? You must have

forgotten your own barbed wire language,
you on the top of buildings you flirt

with jumping off, all those dirty sheets
and shadows. I'm only worthy if I slice

open every hurt I've got inside me, right?
Confess every ugly edge I sharpen

myself with. Yes. There's more
to me than pain, but what does it matter

if no one remembers?

Last Notes

Why do I think so much
of my aunt's last days
that autumn, of her

labored breath,
the oxygen mask,
instead of the brilliant

hues of her life
when it still bloomed?
Her laugh loud

in a beach chair,
book in her hand
and feet in the sand—

the cousin-fests,
her love for chocolate
anything, just like mine,

or when I came out to her
and she said "I am
so proud of you."

We kids would play
Heart and Soul on her
tired piano, some keys

numbed to a dull *ping*,
while my aunts cooked
Thanksgiving dinner.

We held the last notes
under our fingers,
not focused

on how it faded,
just happy
to play a song.

The First Time

For weeks her fingers
lingered. Edged

closer, musicians
tracing the keys.

We both led
and followed,

praised the slick
wet center, the song

we pulled from its strings.
I remember nothing

but the swell of her
skin singing, the sound

of my body saying all
the right things.

WHAT SEPARATES US

The one left out
of the poem. Oldest
and most *different*.
Most books inhaled
alone in her room.
Most trouble
in school, most time
spent with animals.
Most therapy. Most adopted.
Most waiting at the window
for Luke Skywalker. Most
bullied. Most on-the-
spectrum. Most lonely—
always, always most lonely.

A Conversation with My Period

You bitch who overstays
her welcome, your visits
spanning two weeks,
always lingering
at the door before
making your final
exit, lightening
to liner amounts, then
overflowing again
with one last story,
one last point to make.
You always have
so much to say.
I remind you I don't
need you—"Yeah yeah,
no babies for you,"
you say, taking a sip
of your red wine—but still
you return month after
month. I tried a patch
and you laughed, stayed
longer just to spite me.
You are a messy house
guest, staining my bed
sheets, my underwear,
my sweatpants. Worse,
you bring that heavy ache,
unburden your sorrows so I have
no choice but to sink into
them, pick the most gut-
wrenching record and drop
the needle on its skin. "Honey,
let's turn the volume up on
that heartbreak. I can hardly
hear it." So many of my days I bleed
for what I will never carry,
make space for your stories,
your tears, your too-muchness,
your mess, the way you unfasten

all the parts of me I hold
in. I say I can't wait
for the day you stop
showing up. "You'll miss
me," you say. And I almost
believe you. Who else
gives me this permission
to spill out all this sadness?
To make a mess?
To bleed?

Two Days after Roe v. Wade is Overturned, My Wife Cuts Our Hair

It's a hot Arkansas summer Sunday
and you are on our deck in front
of the full-length mirror I'd brought

from inside, wearing only your sports
bra and underwear, to hell with any
neighbors who may step outside and see

your body, to hell with anyone who tells us
what to do with our bodies. This image
is the kind of ordinary that feels holy.

I can already feel myself looking back on it
in some future where you don't live,
and I mean *live* as in this version of you,

the you who now cuts hair pinched between
fingers, the tiny remnants scattered
all over your neck and back, itchy against damp

skin. My hair is mixed with yours on the ground
from where you buzzed it earlier, and I wonder
if birds will use it to make nests, if in this way

we'll help build their homes. The shadows
of branches sway at your feet, across
your skin, all without touching you

at all. Now you hold a small mirror
against the larger one to check your work
from every angle, all the parts you can't

see. Now you pick up the clippers
from the railing again, realizing
your work is not quite done.

WE ARE GATHERED HERE TODAY

Our family sat in the same pew every Sunday.
All six of us in a neat row, admired by
the congregation, who would come up
after the service to tell us

what a beautiful family we were.
Years later, Mom told me she couldn't
stand it, the dissonance. It was then
I most clearly understood the choice

to end her marriage. I'd seen her
as the villain, the one who shattered
the stained-glass window. Now I have
my own family. People comment below

our photos online saying how beautiful
our love is. I can feel the weight, the pressure.
I can put my own fingers on the glass—
understand the impulse to push, to reveal

the mess behind it, a more real
kind of beauty. A window
not to break,
                              but to open.

Revising the Love Poem

I start with a tender moment—dancing
in the kitchen after the funeral. The smell

of her hair, the way she held me. Compare
the blue of her eyes not to the sky or the ocean,

but to hydrangeas, the centerpieces at our wedding,
or that Joni Mitchell album we both love. Cross out

the fight on our honeymoon, the stony silence
as we drove the rental car to the resort—no one wants

to see that. Of course I put the poem in couplets. Break
on words like *want* or *mine* or *hold*. Highlight

the social justice of it all, the "Love Wins!" poster framed
on our living room wall, the rally where men tried to punch

her, my hand pulling her away. I paint us as star-
crossed, our struggle, romantic. Write about sex,

but veil it in metaphor—my hands, voyagers, the freckles
on her back, the night sky. Condense the months we've gone

without touching into a single line: "And then a forest grew
between us." I was not taught to write an ending beyond

happily-ever-after, but I pick up my pen, ready
for whatever happens next.

And You Can Use My Skin
To Bury Secrets In

The first time I use a menstrual cup
and am uncertain if it is in right

you reach inside me, your fingers
circling where they'd been

so many times before, and I know
this is intimacy. My body, so comfortable

in your hands, your hands, so comfortable
in my body and I didn't know

love could be like this, like a car ride
singing along to the same Fiona Apple album,

the one that soundtracked our sadness
years before we met, that it could be a song

I sang alone once, now, with someone else
who has learned every word

of my body, who is not afraid
to reach inside me.

To touch
every part.

My Therapist Says Imagining Your Body Doing Something Has Similar Effects to Actually Doing It

When I say I keep feeling
the urge to dance down
the dark halls after
work, all the empty

classrooms lined up like
an audience, she tells me
to imagine myself doing it.
When I finally tell her

about my college years,
my wrists pinned to dirty
sheets, my "No" swatted
away like the smallest

fly, she asks me to sit with it.
When I say I want to scream
at that first man, she says, "Imagine
you are. Feel it in your throat."

When I say I want to slam
the door in his face as he admits
he always felt bad about what
he did, she says, "Picture it."

Of course, this is a revisionist
history. In reality, I reassured
him. Blamed myself. I tell her
I feel like I've returned to a stage

years after the show ended, my anger
in tow, ready to fucking *dance*, but
everyone else has gone home. It's too late,
the show is over. She says, "Not for you."

BIBLE BELT GAY

My neighbors were forbidden to watch
Disney because the company didn't condemn

"gay" people. It was the first time I ever heard
the word. It coiled inside me, rattled its fire
and brimstone. I didn't understand it

exactly, but knew it was perverse. Fruit
from the tree not to be reached for.

/

During a lunchtime debate, an oboe player
insisted the Bible says gay people are going
to hell. "Well I don't believe in the Bible then,"

I hissed. A silence followed, everyone's eyes wide
and on me. I took it back, felt my face flush

with shame. I understood—I had taken a step
too far from the garden. Looked down and saw
my naked flesh.

/

I only had one boyfriend in high school
and I cringed every time he kissed

my cheek. When I arrived at the dance
on his arm, a girl who often teased me

said, "Good—we were all
starting to wonder about you."

/

A girl I played soccer with had a favorite saying:
"That's so gay." Years later, I watched a home video

and my jaw dropped when I heard the phrase come out
of my own mouth, the camcorder heavy on my shoulder

as I stood in front of a mirror, commenting on how bad
my hair looked in the reflection: "So gay, so gay."

/

My college professor told me about a lesbian student
interviewing for teaching positions. "I told her she needs

to make sure to look a certain way when she interviews,
or she won't get the job." I nodded, still closeted,
but seen.

/

I hadn't been to a church in years, but decided to join
my sister. She assured me the church was progressive.

The preacher started in on Eve, on temptation,
on the importance of keeping marriage sacred—

between a man and a woman.
During the prayer, my sister looked

at me. The old shame tried to slither inside,
but I followed my own commandments by then.

Without a word, we stood up
and walked out before the preacher

could say *Amen.*

My Unborn

You will never be a twinkle
in anyone's eye. It will never
be your turn, your dance

card empty every
month as you sway
in the corner

alone. You will never
be a dancer. Or a painter.
Or a doctor. Or a good

friend. You will never
be. Not accidentally.
Not on purpose

after years of trying
and trying and I could
give you a lifetime

of reasons why, say
the world outside
this body is much

worse, that it doesn't
deserve you. I could say
too many women I love

were betrayed by their own
bodies. My mother waited
so long to grow me—the first

to emerge from her
alive. Maybe while
I grew, I swallowed her

grief. Maybe I love you
too much to lose you.
Maybe I love me

too much. Maybe the truth
is I just don't have time
to watch my stomach swell

with anything other than
indulgence. With more
me. Maybe I have

too many parts
of myself yet
to be born.

GSA

One girl lies and tells her mom she's in a "culture club."
One girl tells us about both times she came out,

the first time, as a gay boy. One student gives us a new
name and pronoun to call them, but only at club meetings.

One made rainbow cupcakes for a bake sale before
her parents banned her from attending. One boy

wears nail polish and eyeliner and reads us his poetry
about boys and manatees. One student gifts us with

a lesson on Black activists, on how intersectionality
means no one gets left out. One girl wears a suit

to prom. One boy hovers at the doorway. One girl
wears a gay-themed shirt everyday—her favorite says

No One Knows I'm a Lesbian. One girl puts up club flyers
even if they get torn down. One boy keeps reminding

us that a Pride day at school is a bad idea, that people
will say things. "I'm just being realistic," he says.

But they put on their rainbow attire anyway. I watch them roam
the halls from my classroom doorway—marquees of color

splashed among the crowd. The day a student asked me
in the middle of class if I was gay I said yes, even

though a teacher at a nearby school was fired for being
a bride with another bride, even though later,

a conservative radio station would post my engagement
photo online like a Wanted poster. Who better

to prepare me, to teach me how to live life outside
of a closet than the same kids who clap every time I say

"my wife?" Who gather around her picture on my desk
like it's a holy grail, who are so desperate for heroes,

they wear pride flags tied around their necks as capes,
become the heroes themselves.

You Tell Our Therapist We Got into a Fight Because I Wanted to Pop Your Zit and You Wouldn't Let Me

and you told her, even though I specifically asked you
not to, and isn't this so typical, my shame at all

the gross ways I try to squeeze out the truth,
the tension, how I'm forever trying to open

you up, and will I ever get used to all of this
need on display? Parts of me that explode

out and streak down
my face. Our therapist says

the silly fights are never about
what they seem, that the problem

is underneath, that we must bring it
to the surface. But what happens

when what's inside makes
a mess on our mirror,

one we can't clean up?
What happens when we

have to stare at it every day,
these parts of us we can never

put back inside?

THE CONDITIONAL

If your gender was a secret—
        a lost child who wouldn't tell us

their name. If the child would lie
        between us in bed.

If we hadn't touched
        in months. If my hands

ached from the not
        touching. If they longed

to touch a woman. If I was
        a woman who loved

women. If you were no longer
        a woman. If we were once

wives who became something
        else. If you said "I know you

didn't sign up for this." If I still
        loved you. If I told myself

"It's about love, not gender." If I knew
        that was the truth, but not

the whole truth. If my desire was
        also a child, one I could no longer

feed. If we loved these two
        children, our miraculous

conceptions we spent years giving
        birth to, the only life we'd felt grow

inside us, if to keep them meant
        to lose each other. If we had to

choose.

Venom

My first classroom was at the end
of the hall. My teacher desk sat on
a platform that I sometimes tripped
on when I'd write on the board,
and the day we read a Medusa
poem, a tiny snake emerged from
its worn carpet, my ninth graders

suddenly tittering with excitement.
I wouldn't let anyone touch it, emptied
a trashcan and put it top-down on
the snake, a makeshift cage, and evacuated
my students outside while the principal
took care of the unwelcome visitor.

That was the year my students acted out
Romeo and Juliet, learned the lines
by heart. All day I watched Romeos
mime drinking poison and slump
dramatically on the classroom floor
moments before Juliet opened her eyes.

That was the year a boy asked to speak
to me in the hall. He shifted from one foot
to the other, wrung his hands, said he needed
to tell me something, said I seemed like a person
he could talk to, and before I could process
what was happening, I told him I was

a "mandated reporter," that I had to report
if he was in danger, from himself or others,
and the boy's mouth closed, and he said
"Never mind," and no matter how I tried
to reassure him, he wouldn't talk to me.
A week later, he stopped coming to school.

When I talked to the counselors, they said
there was nothing they could do. I will always
wonder about the harm I did that day, the words

I stopped him from saying—I will always regret
the poison of my fear.

SECONDS

Thanksgiving. My grandmother has buried a husband
for the second time. We load our plates, heavy, when a cry stabs

the chatter. Her wordless grief-song echoes in the kitchen.
I play chase with my mother's eyes, but she is busy

with her plate, scooping an extra serving of mashed potatoes,
refilling her glass of wine. The house burns.

We sit down to eat as my aunt hushes my grandmother out
the door and drives her home. We pretend not to notice.

Our throats never vessel such sounds. We eat until our faces
reflect on shiny clean plates. No one goes back for seconds.

When Our Cat Had Kittens

What if, instead of carrying
a child, I am supposed to carry grief?
                    —Ada Limón

They all started dying. Feline leukemia,
the vet later said. We buried the first
in a sock, an ankle one that felt
impossibly small. When only

one cat remained, my older sister
lit candles, draped the small kitten
in her crystal necklace, held on as tightly
as she could before the inevitable

loss. How fragile they each were,
these closed-eyed visitors, deaths
like candles on a birthday
cake blown out one

by one, before anyone could
make a wish. What I remember
best but try to forget is the way
their mother kept returning

to that cabinet in the garage
where she'd given birth,
as if she was looking

for her babies, as if she hoped
they would be there waiting.

COMMUNITY THEATER

Backstage there were remnants of other worlds—
a drawbridge to a castle, creaking stairs that led
nowhere, a crescent moon lightless and looming
on the stone wall. At dress rehearsals or opening
nights, the powder smell of heavy makeup followed
me down the halls, my hair stiff with spray, my feet
bare and quiet, careful not to break the hushed holy
as we waited. And waited. It seemed it was never
our time to come out, to emerge from these half-worlds.

There was a girl who hid in the costume room.
Together, we pulled out suit jackets and suspenders,
parts we weren't meant to play, tried on different roles.
Shyly, I watched her dress, taking note of the outfits
she picked. I came back later and tried them on alone,
running my hands over the fabric as I looked down
and imagined my hands belonged to someone else.

ANXIOUS ATTACHMENT

I need you to hold me
in the exact right way.
You must remember your lines.
When the tension fills the room

in the exact right way,
be ready for my monologue.
When the tension fills the room
like a swelling orchestra of strings,

be ready for my monologue.
I need you to say you love me
like a swelling orchestra of strings
at the exact right time, before

I need you to say you love me
or I'll see the flicker of the reel
at the exact right time, before
it rips across the screen,

or I'll see the flicker of the reel
even if it's not really there.
It rips across the screen—
I'll swear there's something wrong,

even if it's not really there.
I need you to hold me.
I'll swear there's something wrong.
You must remember your lines.

SCIENTISTS SAY THE TITANIC WILL DISAPPEAR IN 20 YEARS

Footage of the Titanic's departure shows passengers swarmed her
decks to say farewell. Women waved handkerchiefs across
the railing, any voice or sound drowned in silent film.
What's more haunting is her body abandoned on the ocean
floor—all those ballrooms once filled with laughter
and dancing, now an empty tomb fish float across
like ghosts. Now a crushed piano, its keys crooked
teeth in a broken smile, a portrait of decay. Rust-
icicles form a beard across the ship's face,
which now we know is the sign of her
second death, the metal-eating bacteria
that every day makes her smaller.
This is an iceberg we can see coming,
but are just as powerless to stop. Is it more
graceful, more gentle, this death? How many
ways are there to disappear? In my classroom,
a book vanishes from the shelf. A rainbow
sticker is torn from the wall. Every day
I walk in and find I have become
smaller. I pause before I mention
my wife. I pretend the news doesn't
exist. I wear a Black Lives Matter
pin on my lanyard but never
say the words out loud. I am impartial
to the point of invisibility. It is more
than empty ballrooms, than the way
my body is becoming see-through,
how my rust-beard drags the floor.
More than the iceberg we see
coming, that is already here.
It's not even that it may be
too late to pull myself
to the surface and have
any part of me left.
It's that I don't
think I'll like
what remains.

Self-Portrait in Which I Am a Spider and My Fear Is a Web

A spider is suspended
between our cars

big as my thumb,
as if it is floating

in mid-air. The web
winks in the early

morning sun—not
just a strand draped

across the driveway,
but an entire tapestry,

intricate and beautiful,
all spun while we were

sleeping. Imagine her
careful weaving

in the dark as the moon
waned into daylight,

this laborious construction,
this tether that I must

break.

III.

SOMETHING NEW

PORTRAIT OF A MARRIAGE

Is love posing
for the portrait?

Trusting your
person to see

your every
flaw, to put

paint to
canvas,

to somehow
make it both

beautiful
and true?

And don't
I capture

us here
on the page,

stubborn proof,
for better

or worse,
again and

again?
And when

death
parts us,

won't these words
remain?

IF I HAD THREE LIVES

After Sarah Russell

I'd marry you in two. In the other, I'd come
out in college, date a woman in a rock band
who pushes me against the grungy wall

at one of her shows and kisses me. I'd date
a poet I meet in a coffee shop whose flannel
shirts smell like burnt vanilla. We'd stay up

reading each other Mary Oliver and smoking
cigarettes. I'd fall in love, then out of it. I'd take
my broken heart to New York City, be broke

in an apartment I share with two others. We'd stay
up drinking cheap wine on the rooftop, laugh and bitch
and share our deepest wants and fears. I'd scrap

my way through the city, try to make it
as a writer, spend sleepless nights looking
for adventure, finding it in art and friends

and love and myself, never knowing
I was looking for you all along.

HOW SHE LOVED US

My mother was not fooled
by thermometers held closely
to a lamp's bulb, was unimpressed
when the school nurse would call

about our "low grade" fevers.
But one morning when I was overcome
with a sadness I do not remember
the root of, she broke

her rule. I sat across from her
at the kitchen counter as she called
the school, told them I wasn't feeling
well and "had a rash," at which point

she smiled at me conspiratorially,
proud of her half-truth since
my face was covered with red
blotches from the intensity of my tears.

I don't know that I've ever felt
so held, which is maybe why
the memory shines brightly
in my mind: My mother showing me

every feeling deserves to take
space, that there is room
for all of this beauty and blunder.
There is room for all of me.

THINGS THAT COULD BE SAID ABOUT BOTH DIVORCE AND LEAVING TEACHING

Think of the children. It's not meant to be
easy. But you seemed so happy. You were

made for this. I just thought you were in it for
the long haul. You're so good together. Every

relationship has problems. Have you tried
counseling? I just always saw you

together. What else will you do? You made
a promise. It's not meant to be

so hard. I don't know how you made it
this long. You deserve more. Love
shouldn't be so painful. Good

for you. There's a whole world
on the other side of this grief—just

hold on. It gets so much better.
I'm proud of you. I know how hard
you tried. Someday, it won't hurt

so much. It's okay to remember
the good times. You need to take time

to heal. You deserve to feel safe. To feel
loved. Someday, this will all make
sense. You'll look back and understand

why it could never work out. You are not
a failure. Sometimes leaving

is coming home to yourself. How brave
to make that change. To choose
you. What a good example

you are setting.
Think of the children.

When I Think of Parenthood

I think of my grandfather in the ICU.
How when my father and I were visiting him

and about to leave, he begged my father to call him
after he made it home safely. He'd cried the time

my father's phone died as he was driving home,
called me in a panic, sure something had happened.

But ICU rooms have no phones. Just a window to a dark
sky. A curtain for privacy. Just the flashing lights of a silent

TV. The sound of my grandfather's labored breath through
the oxygen mask the doctors made him wear, but he kept

taking off. So, on the way out, we asked the nurse to wait
thirty minutes, then to pretend we had called her, asked her

to go in and tell my ninety-seven-year-old grandfather
that his boy made it home.

MAGIC TRICKS

My sister and I begged him to let us
ride our bikes to school all year.

It's what kids in books and movies did—
rode off on adventures, racing

down the streets with their friends,
But our elementary school was too far

and across a busy highway. We were not
the kind of kids with cards pinned

to our wheel spokes, bells cheerfully
announcing our every arrival

and departure. Most of the time, we kept
to the small circles of our driveway.

But on my last day of fourth grade,
Dad loaded our bikes into the back

of his blue truck and drove us across
the highway, keeping a careful eye

on our bikes jostling in the back. He stopped
at the bottom of the hill leading up to the school,

took out our bikes and said, "Go ahead."
My sister and I began the long trek up that hill,

our handlebars wavering as we stood up
in our seats with the effort. He drove behind us,

waved every annoyed and honking car past us
with a flick of his wrist out the window, his own

bit of magic. My father, who may not always
understand or have the words to say, but when curtains

open, he will always appear, face in the audience
at my readings, car pulling into my older sister's driveway

that impossible year, his truck crawling at our heels
as we shakily make our way forward.

My Unborn: An Erasure

You   twinkle
in

                              this body

                    say

          grow me

      Maybe
I   allowed

grief
too much

        Maybe
  I   have time

      yet

I Read That to Love Someone Long Term Is to Attend a Thousand Funerals of the People They Used to Be

Here lies the long-haired girl at the dive bar
playing beer pong on the night we met, the one

who crawled into bed with me when I was sick, blamed
food poisoning instead of me as she knelt by the toilet

the next day. Here lies our rose-colored-glasses, our fear
of honesty. Here lies the time she taught me to cook,

my inexperience endearing, her guidance, welcomed.
The sliced sweet potatoes in the pan, the way they looked

like carrots but weren't. Here lies the night she pressed me
against my car and kissed me and a man walked by

and leered at us, but she shielded me with her body
and I'd never felt more safe. Here lies the woman

they were, the night they shaved their head and then
helped me shave part of mine, our bodies covered

with tiny hairs, parts of us we shed like snakeskin.
Their new pronouns, new label—here lies my fear

that our love couldn't survive such a change.
Here lies the day they ran through

a field at my mother's and it took them twenty
damn times to fly the kite, but they never gave up—

adjusted the strings and their run and kept going
until it flew. Here lies my doubt. Here lies

the first love poem, a seed that keeps sprouting
into something new. Here lies every choice that led us

here. All the selves we were,
and all those that have yet to bloom.

PRACTICING
After Marie Howe

I want to write a love poem for the couple
who sat outside the vet's office with their dog

on a picnic blanket, on the one scrap of grass
A song for the dog's slow saunter that would be

his last as the tech came to lead him away, his fur
gray, his tail down, and how the couple watched

him leave and immediately wept. They held each
other for several minutes in front of a row of cars

all witnesses to their grief, I among them, thinking
of my own dog inside getting his shots, and it felt

private and personal but still I watched, and it was
practicing. And I thought of the year in junior high

my English teacher's son died in a car crash.
The first time I saw her after the incident

was buffet night at the pizza place. Her usual
vibrant curls were lifeless, straight,

framing her face. She held her plate
against her chest as she approached

the buffet as if there was nothing there
she wanted. Her eyes scanned the room

and landed on mine, and I ran back
to my table, empty plate in hand, willing

to go hungry. At the vet, I kept watching
the couple. I kept practicing, until they wiped

their eyes. Got into their empty
car. I want to write a song for the quiet

as they drove away.

I Now Pronounce You

We start with the dog,
who is misgendered

so often, it feels only
natural to refer to them

as "they." At home
we practice: "Look!

They are being so sweet,"
I say when Bug lays their

head on my lap. "We need
to give them a bath," you say

after sniffing their spotted
fur, your nose wrinkling

a bit. Soon I start to try
out your pronouns, too.

On the phone with
my sister, at dinner

with a friend. It begins
to feel like second

nature, like a photograph
coming into focus, one

I didn't realize was blurry.
Like all this time I'd been

mispronouncing your name
and finally said it right.

ODE TO MY WIFE'S GENDER

My dearest theyby. You magician
with kitchen scissors, coming out

of the bathroom with the coolest cut.
Praise your toolbelt and the way

you wear it. Praise the evolution
of your pronouns and your closet,

dresses replaced with blazers,
button-ups, shiny black boots.

My heart bursts when you are bow-tied
and beaming in hot pink pants. Praise

your hands on a guitar or hammer or my
thigh. Praise the purple toy car

proudly displayed on our shelf—
the afterthought birthday present

from your dad after you'd opened
all the Barbies and bows, after you blew

out your five candles and wished yourself
a boy, like you did every year. Praise

your joy at being seen. Praise your tears
at the dog commercial, or the movie

Wall-E, or when you play *500 Miles*
on the guitar and sing it next to me.

Praise your crooked grin. The arch
of your eyebrow that punctuates

your speech in perfect rhythm when you're
telling me a story. Praise the way you cradle

our little dog and sway with him

in the kitchen, his tail wagging

then pick up all sixty pounds
of our other dog and do the same.

Praise the way you dance—free,
shirt untucked, the last one

on the dance floor. Praise
how you grab my hand

to join you, the way you lead
and follow in equal measure.

HOME VIDEOS

Here the dead blink and the screen
blinks back. Stripes flicker across
my grandmother's face as she
watches us play in the living
room. Here my younger sister crawls
after me, coos her round vowels
into the air. Here my older sister
is always alone, pretending
she is Peter Pan. Here I dance
on command, sing into the toy
microphone my dad holds for me,
loops of *Twinkle Twinkle Little Star.*
Here my brother is a stranger buried
in my mother. Here it is her hands
that hold the camera. Here no cancer
or divorce. New York or funerals.
No miles or years or worlds
that separate us. The screen
flickers, blinks, will always tell
only part of the story.

A Week after My Grandfather's Funeral

I found my father
at his parents' house

on his knees and weeping
in front of a baby photo

of his mother. It was hand-tinted
which made my grandmother doll-like,

her face rosy, lips red and full
of life. She was ten years

gone, her ashes just buried
with my grandfather's body.

But this picture made
the grief new, breathed

life into its cheeks. Through
his tears, my dad said

"She was such a pretty baby."
He had never known her

like that. I thought it strange
this was what broke him, not

a photo with a face he could
remember, arm in arm with

his father or smiling next to
his sister on Christmas morning.

Instead, it was her at the beginning,
still a stranger, still with her life

ahead, yet to meet her son
who would one day mourn her

here, parentless
and kneeling at the altar

of her life after
it ended, before it began.

When My Mother Was Born, She Was Already Carrying the Egg That Would Become Me

I was there when she made mud pies,
earned the nickname Tilly the Toiler

on her grandparents' farm.
I was there the first time

she touched a horse, the pink
of its nose soft under her hand.

I was there when she was
on homecoming court, wore

the paisley dress. When she wrote
the poem about how she felt

she was playing a role, that no one
really knew her, and they published it

in the school paper. I was there
when she drove her friend

to the abortion clinic. I was there
when her father told her to become

a nurse. There the first time she held
the hand of a patient who was dying.

I was there when she kissed my father
under the magnolia tree, her lace gown

pooled around her feet—there when they lost
the first baby. And the second,

and the third. And before she was
Mother. Wife. Before I wrote

my own poems, I was there, and I still
didn't see her.

The Only Part I Remember about Our Trip to Disney World

is missing our flight. My mother did not hold back.
She dropped her bags and collapsed into the nearest
chair, wept openly, her face in her hands with the kind

of abandon we didn't ever see from her. It was then I saw
my mom as human, and by human, I mean someone
who wept. Who mourned and wanted and had

disappointments too big to carry. It felt like the world
had shifted, could crumble. The flight attendant avoided
our eyes. My father hung back. My brother wrapped
his small arms around my mother's neck. Now, I am

listening to the dogs' quiet breaths at my feet. The sheer
curtains glow in the afternoon sun beside me. My empty
plate sits on the desk. I am looking back at this moment

and telling my mother it is okay to cry, to cry as loudly
as she wants. I am running down the airport terminal, prying
open the doors. I am fixing this one thing. I am leading
my father to my mother and joining their hands.
They walk down the terminal together,
and the four of us follow.

A Toast

Today we drink champagne
for breakfast, straight

from the bottle. Fry eggs
and use the spatula

as a microphone.
Dance when the song

demands to be danced to.
You kiss me between

laughter and we overcook
the eggs.

This week I picked a dress
for our wedding

and one for a funeral.

I know it should feel wrong,
to dance, but nothing

feels more necessary than to take
another slice of champagne, spin you

around and pull you in close, bury
my face in your hair.

Let the toast
burn.

The Weekend after the Club Q Shooting

My wife and I walk our dogs.
We watch an award show

on our couch, bicker a bit about
money. We make plans. Make lists—

what to clean out of our garage, ideas
for a living room remodel. Plans

for me to carry our child, for my
wife's top surgery, for more

life. A braver life. We turn
the heat on to fight against

the cold. We tuck ourselves
into our warm bed, let the dogs

up with us as a treat. We say
goodnight with the knowledge

that tomorrow we will wake up
together, with the knowledge

that so many won't. In the face
of the goddamn tragedy of it all,

the grief we hold collectively,
that some hold in unspeakable

volumes tonight, what else is there
for us to do but this?

ODE TO MY HEART

You mother of this wavering
    pulse. You warmonger

waving white flags, bouquet
    of contradictions. You river-

maker. Ship with a thousand
    sails. Fist filled

with every person I love.
    You engine,

percussion of panic
    and joy, cadence

of grief—you slow march
    to sleep. You messy

conductor of a reckless
    song, radio playing

every station at once.
    You mouth attempting

to hold in the ocean.
    You ocean. Wave after

wave, the hush
    of always this rhythm,

this cycle, water
    meets shore, then un-

becomes once more, back
    and back—you womb.

You who keeps breaking
    open.

PRAYER
After Nicole Homer

God of planning. God of two-point-five children smiling in the perfect

Christmas cards, photos strewn across the fridge like string

lights. God of white dresses and white picket fences.

The two-car garage. The football games. God of gender

reveals, of balloon arches and frosting. God of pink

and blue. God of uncomfortable family reunions.

God of pronouns. God of avoiding them. God of changing

them. God of change. God of me proposing, but taking

your name. God of balance, of losing balance, of finding it

again. God of labels: wife, lesbian, nonbinary, queer, family

values. God of family. Ours. God of ours. God of never

stepping foot in a church. God of we are our own church.

God of we are our own. God of our Christmas card,

just the two of us, our only children the dogs.

God of we are enough. God of let us gay up

your fridge. God of let's stop trying to fit

inside any box but this.

I Could Lose You

Unless we are like my great-grandparents—
Papa, who took a turn while in the hospital

and died suddenly while Memaw fell asleep
knitting at home that same night and never

woke up. Neither ever lived knowing
the other was gone, a joint funeral, two

caskets buried side by side. And maybe
it's better to live with this wild hope

that we could cheat the universe
out of our loss. If I knew

I could lose you, but also that I could
keep you. That one day, I could close

my eyes, and never open them
in a world without you.

The (Un)Conditional

If your gender was a catalyst

    that set us both free.

If my queerness was a house

    with more rooms than I knew.

If I didn't have to fit. If my fear

    was a liar. If we made our own

rules. If our love was a nesting doll

    we kept opening, if we kept becoming

more of ourselves. If our lives were not bound

    to the path we were shown. If the paths

were endless, grew in every direction

    like the branches of a tree. If we could

choose.

When You Decided the Peach Tree that Produced No Fruit and Took Up the Sunniest Spot of the Yard Had to Go

You sawed at the trunk for more than an hour—
three times you thought you'd managed it, stood

yelling a "Timber!" that got less enthusiastic each time.
Finally, the tree crackled under your weight, groaned

as it fell. That's when you saw the baby bird tucked
inside the trunk. We mourned what we had not known

was being destroyed. Then you got to work. Sawed off
the branch that held life inside it, a chickadee,

and strapped it to a nearby tree, the parents circling
and crying as you worked. After, we went inside

and watched from the window, unsure if what was broken
could be repaired. We remembered the myth that baby birds

are abandoned by their parents when humans get too near.
I imagined a possible future—you fishing out the body

from the branch, your head bowed, burying
the small creature in our backyard. Remembered

all the birds you've found on sidewalks before
and your attempts to save them—all the life you held

in your hands, only to watch it extinguish. Soon the birds
found their relocated nest, fluttered inside to their baby,

and what a gift it was to be able to witness the future you broke
and rebuilt, the new ending you managed to write.

EVIDENCE OF TIME PASSING

The fade of tattoos.

Dust. New words

my students say, clunky

in my mouth. The sour

smell of aged books. Flecks

of white in my wife's hair.

The hangover's zeal. The rot

of trash. My jeans that will

no longer button—my hair

longer. Growth. The dirty

clothes pile. Sore feet after

a day of standing. The ache.

The ache gone. The gentle

way I speak to

myself. Forgiveness.

On Growth

The morning of your top surgery,
you tend to your plants with careful
attention. Fill your watering can

and visit each pot by the windows,
inspecting leaves between gentle

fingers, your body silhouetted against
early light. You take scissors to cut
what's dead away. These cuts are necessary

for the plant to keep growing. To be
healthy. Sometimes, you take

the pieces and put them in water
until they root, until they become
their own.

Recessional

I Now Pronounce You

I now pronounce you your own. Give you back
your names, put down those titles: *Mother, Father,*

Wife, Husband. I pronounce you whole. Better
apart, but still better for once having found each

other. I pronounce you human. Both the stove
and the hand that touches it, if only to learn

what burns. I pronounce your every scar
well earned, roads on a worn map you used

to find your way home. I pronounce you home
and road. Minute and hour hand, together

briefly, moving forward. I pronounce you
the golden leaf and its inevitable

fall. I pronounce you deserving of space
to change, the hydrangea moved

from its pot into earth, roots stretched out
like an unclenched fist. I pronounce you worthy

of looking back with gentle eyes. Both the one
who held me in the backseat, my bleeding

knee in your lap, and the steady hand that drove
us to the hospital. I pronounce you both free

and forever bound, your four children stitched
between you like the binding of a book sewed

together by hand. I pronounce you the pages
and the cover that encases them.

Both the story I know
and the one you wrote without me.

Acknowledgements & Notes

Immense gratitude to the following journals that published these poems first, often in earlier forms.

Germ Magazine: "How She Loved Us"

Brave Voices: "The Only Girl Out at My High School"

Porcupine Literary: "On Being a Closeted Teacher," "Scientists Say the Titanic Will Disappear in 20 Years," "Venom," "Things That Could Be Said about Both Divorce and Leaving Teaching"

SWWIM: "I Now Pronounce You"

Nimrod International Journal: "Broken Ghazal," "Bible Belt Gay," "Ode to My Wife's Gender," "When I Think of Parenthood"

Preposition: "June 26th, 2015" (Later titled "The World's Smallest Pride Parade")

Stonewall Fifty from Sibling Rivalry Press: "GSA"

The Legendary: "Seconds"

Barrelhouse: "And You Can Use My Skin To Bury Secrets In"

Lavender Review: "I Read that to Love Someone Long Term is to Attend a Thousand Funerals of the People They Used to Be"

Glass: A Journal of Poetry: "A Toast"

Screen Door Review: "When You Decided the Peach Tree that Produced No Fruit and Took Up the Sunniest Spot of the Yard Had to Go," "Prayer," "When My Mother Was Born, She Was Already Carrying the Egg That Would Become Me," "The First Time," "Ode to My Heart"

Thank you to Sibling Rivalry Press, who published these poems in my chapbook, *Lesbian Fashion Struggles:* "The Only Girl Out at My High School," "GSA," and "A Toast."

The title "And You Can Use My Skin To Bury Secrets In" is taken from Fiona Apple's song, "I Know."

The title "I Read that to Love Someone Long Term is to Attend a Thousand Funerals of the People They Used to Be" is from Heidi Priebe.

THANKS

Thank you to Derrick Brown and Nikki Steele—being part of the Write Bloody family is a dream come true. Thanks for all you do to create this space for readers and writers, for reminding the world that poetry is alive and well.

Thank you to Sam Rose Preminger—you are the best editor and supporter I could have asked for in this process. Thank you for your sharp eye and kind heart. I'm so glad we got to work on this project together. Also thank you to Wess Mongo Jolley for your proofreading expertise and guidance in giving this manuscript such careful polishing before publication.

Thank you to Megan Falley for your mentorship and continued support—the opening poem in this book was the first one we ever worked on together, and it was a transformative experience for me. Thank you for rooting for me.

Thank you to Desireé Dallagiacomo for all the spaces you create for writers to share their words and hearts. I'm so grateful for my time in Undercurrent; many of these poems were born in that group.

Thank you to Kai Coggin, Lisa Summe, Susie Dumond, and Sierra DeMulder, firstly for writing books that were lanterns on my way to writing my own, and secondly for generously agreeing to write blurbs.

Thank you to Hannah Beresford and Rosebud Ben-Oni for looking at an early version of the manuscript and helping give my revisions direction. And thank you to Hannah for suggesting the book title! That was a game-changer.

A special shoutout to Laurel Page for your friendship and feedback. I am a better writer because of you. Also thank you to Katy Mullins for giving me such good perspective and advice—your early hunch that I should lean into my poems about parenthood in this manuscript was spot on!

Thank you to my writing group for giving feedback on so many of these poems: Ashley Steineger, Chelsea Risley, Courtney LeBlanc, Barbara Costas-Biggs, and Amy Haddad.

Thank you to the QLCA Book Club, particularly the original members Alecia, Emma, Jeryca, Melinda, and Sam, for your support and communion, for the holy space we've created. I could talk gay shit with y'all all day.

Thank you to the friends who have continually supported me as a writer and a human— Ellie, Heather, Bethany, Ali, Melissa, Lisa, and Colton.

Thank you to Jenn Terrell (JET) for taking my author photo, and thank you to Rock Town Roller Derby for helping me learn to take up space and find my voice.

Thank you to every therapist I've worked with, especially for the time one told me, "It's never too late to heal a wound."

Thank you to my parents for your graciousness in this process—writing this book, sharing it with you, and having the conversations that followed was incredibly healing for me. I'm so grateful you gave me that gift. I couldn't ask for better parents.

Thank you to my siblings: To Mary, for your wisdom and unwavering support and love. To Lizzie, for going on this healing journey with me and so often leading the way. To Thomas, for your huge heart and willingness to keep showing up for those you love. I love each of you beyond measure. I'm so proud to be your sister.

Thank you to my wife Bonnie for being my editor, my cheerleader, my muse. For diving with me into the tough stuff, and for making me feel safe enough to go there. For trusting me to write about it. Thanks for living your most authentic life, and inspiring me to be my bravest and best self. Thanks for loving me so well.

ABOUT THE AUTHOR

Caroline Earleywine is a poet and educator who spent ten years teaching high school English in Central Arkansas. She's a Pushcart Prize and Best of the Net nominee, was a 2021 finalist for Nimrod's Pablo Neruda Prize for Poetry, and has work in Glass: A Journal of Poetry, Barrelhouse, NAILED Magazine, and elsewhere. She earned her MFA from Queens University in Charlotte and her chapbook, Lesbian Fashion Struggles, was published with Sibling Rivalry Press in 2020. I Now Pronounce You is her first full-length collection. She lives in Little Rock with her wife and two dogs. You can keep up with her work at carolineearleywine.com.

If You Like Caroline Earleywine, Caroline Likes...

Drive Here and Devastate Me
Megan Falley

Pansy
Andrea Gibson

Racing Hummingbirds
Jeanann Verlee

The Smell of Good Mud
Lauren Zuniga

Glitter in the Blood: A Poet's Manifesto for Better, Braver Writing
Mindy Nettifee

Write Bloody Publishing publishes and promotes great books of poetry every year.
We believe that poetry can change the world for the better. We are an independent press
dedicated to quality literature and book design, with an office
in Los Angeles, California.

We are grassroots, DIY, bootstrap believers. Pull up a good book and join the family.
Support independent authors, artists, and presses.

Want to know more about Write Bloody books, authors, and events?
Join our mailing list at

www.writebloody.com

WRITE BLOODY BOOKS

Printed in the USA
CPSIA information can be obtained
at www.ICGtesting.com
CBHW022145120424
6677CB00004BB/16

9 781949 342550